I0142119

All Scripture references taken from the KJV of the Holy Bible, unless otherwise indicated.

Love Breaks Your Heart

by Dr. Marlene Miles

Freshwater Press 2024

freshwaterpress9@gmail.com

ISBN: 978-1-963164-86-2

Paperback Version

Table of Contents

Every Old Testament prophecy was part of
the Love Letter from God to us.

Dear Beloved

I'm sending you Someone. I'm sending
you Help. I will not leave your soul in hell.
I'm sending you Hope. You will not
remain spiritually dead, even though I
told you (all) not to eat of that tree and
that you would surely die. I'm so sorry
you had to die spiritually, so I'm sending
you Life.

I'm so sorry you had to die.

I miss you.

I'm sending you help from the sanctuary.

I'm sending you LOVE.

Your Father

Love Breaks Your Heart

Freshwater

Freshwater Press, USA

Invocation

Father, we glorify You. We thank You for this word. We thank You, Lord, that You sent Jesus to die in propitiation for our sins. And we bless You for it, in the Name of Jesus.

Thank You for those with ears to hear. Open their understanding and open their eyes that they may see You and hear You, and be changed by this Word, in the Name of the Lord Jesus Christ we pray, Amen Amen.

Love Breaks In

Love breaks *into* a heart.

It seems that when you were least suspecting or expecting such a thing, here comes Love. Love is smooth, sometimes it comes via a smooth talker or a smooth operator, but here it comes. I was not expecting or looking for Love, but gradually or suddenly Love breaks in.

Even with advanced notice, Love *breaks in.* I say that because it makes you change. Love makes you change your mindset and your plans. You end up changing yourself because real Love is a Power, it is a force. If you believe you are in love, but you've not changed and nothing has changed about you, then that is wimpy love--, *fake* love.

Real Love may come in by force, it marches right in through the front door. Even if it has to break in, it will always come in the right way--, through the front door. Love is the greatest power of all because God is Love, therefore Love with no power is not Love at all.

Fake love comes in by any means; it is sneaky, and that is one of the ways you know it is fake.

Period.

Love Breaks Your Heart

Love breaks your heart.

There's an older R&B song that says, *Love breaks your heart and love takes no less than **everything**.*

Love breaks your heart.

And the glory which thou gavest me I have given them; that they may be one, even as we are one:

I in them, and thou in me, that they may be made perfect in one; and that the world may know that thou hast sent me, and hast loved them, as thou hast loved me.

Father, I will that they also, whom thou hast given me, be with me where I am; that they may behold my glory, which thou hast given me: for thou lovedst me before the foundation of the world.

O righteous Father, the world hath not known thee: but I have known thee, and these have known that thou hast sent me.

And I have declared unto them thy name, and will declare it: that the love wherewith thou hast loved me may be in them, and I in them.
(John 17:22-26)

Love breaks your heart because of the **power** of Love. No heart is able to contain Love, therefore the heart breaks to enlarge itself to be able to receive even a little more Love than was there before.

If you put new wine in an old wineskin, that old wineskin will break. Put Love in an existing heart, just like it is, and that heart will be **bursting with Love**. Now, when God is involved in this Love, the heart may break, but God binds up broken hearts, so the Love is accepted, it is good, it is not painful. That heart is bound and kept safe by the hands of God as it adjusts to Love. As it adjusts to the new Power that is in you now.

This is why you need a heart of flesh because it can be bound and healed. The heart of stone, the hardened heart cannot be healed, it stays shattered.

What shall you do with this new power? When someone falls in love with you, they are, in essence, giving you power over them and yet trusting you with it. When you fall in love with someone the same thing happens.

Lovest Thou Me?

Our Lord says, *"Lovest thou me?"* (John 21:15-16). The Lord is using the term *agape*. The first step, the foundation of being able to Love anyone is to first Love God. God is Love and all Love comes from God. If this thing you call Love does not come from God, then it is not real Love. There are perversions of Love, there is counterfeit love, and there is "love" that is not love at all.

Simon Peter answers, " Yea, Lord; thou knowest that I love thee."

The Word here is from the *phileo* the brotherly *love*, and *storge* the familial kind of love. There are other categories, but we will stay with these four for this volume.

Agape is the strongest, most powerful, all-encompassing kind of Love. *Phileo* is brotherly love or affection. You know how it is with siblings--, I love you today but if you take my toy, we may be enemies tomorrow. *Agape* loves always, at all times, and through all things. It is the Love where you **choose** to love, no matter what. *Phileo* is a personal attachment and affection, and in some instances, it is chosen for you and forced upon you.

By whom?

By your parents. I'm sure you remember them saying things such as, *Now, son, that's your sister, you need to love her. Give her a hug and tell her that you're sorry* You weren't even sorry, but you did it anyway.

Phileo love is the kind you might have for your classmates in school, so you don't get into fights with them. That's the one you should have with coeds and coworkers.

There are other kinds of love, but the one we seem to know too much about and hardly anything at all about at the same time is *eros*, which is sexual, romantic, passionate love. Standing on its own, all alone, it is the one that gets folks in all kinds of trouble. That is the one that most secular love songs are written about. That is the one that can change faster than the weather. That one is flesh-driven, and we can wonder if it is *love* at all.

A fellow once told me that people don't know what Love is. I believe he may have been either referring to this kind of love, or taking note that those whom he was talking to, or dating were speaking of this kind of love--, believing it was Love, real Love and there was no other.

This is the love that deception can be easily woven into. *Eros* will protect you from NOTHING, that's why I label it as the weakest since although it is the most prevalent, it is the "trouble-love." As a matter of fact, it is the trap; somehow the devil gets into this kind the most because flesh is involved in it—and flesh to the max, if a couple is in sin.

Agape is the Love that has the power to keep you, protect you, surround you, and bless you. ***Agape* gives.**

Eros takes.

Phileo is somewhat in between and more or less neutral. Phileo and eros can both mask other motives as household folks let their guard down when they believe *phileo* is in play and they are in a safe environment. But, are they? After all, a brother is born for adversity.

Love breaks your heart. Which "love" has the power to do that?

Perhaps they all do.

Let's look at the *Love Chapter*, 1 Corinthians 13.

And they shall know you by the Love you show to one another. Love often is what you saw growing up or what you saw on TV or at the movies. Sometimes Love is what is described in the pop music you listen to.

None of that could really be Love.

According to 1 Corinthians, Love appears to be an attitude, but it is either the

Holy Spirit in action or it is a collection of other spirits that provoke action or inaction in a person. Love can constrain you. Love can motivate you. Love may restrain you from acting out when you need to remain calm.

Love is patient.

Love is kind.

Right off the bat we see that Love precludes works of the flesh; so the acting out is off the table right away. Love is the aggregation of the Fruit of the Spirit--, as said, *Agape* Love is the Holy Spirit in action.

Love does not dishonor or disrespect others. It is not self-seeking, or easily angered. Love keeps no list of wrongs done--, so that means that Love forgives, probably often and easily.

Love covers a multitude of sins; it does not gossip. The Word says it doesn't delight in evil, either doing it or talking about it. We all know that talking about evil is gossip. This writer believes that gossip is witchcraft; so, don't do it.

Love always protects, always trusts, always hopes. Love shores up the spirit of a man; Love always perseveres. When you may want to lose heart, you can't, and you don't because of Love.

Love is a **power**; it is the greatest power; therefore, Love never fails.

Christians often think that Love and being loving means being a pushover or giving in all the time to keep the peace. That is not Love, either. Love is a Power; it is stronger than anything. How can that which is the strongest be a pushover? You take a parent who is defending their child or other loved one, they will rise up on their opponent full force because of Love.

God will contend with those who contend with you. That's because of Love.

No matter how smart I am, if I don't have Love, I'm nothing. No matter how impressive I sound standing at a microphone or how sweet I may sound whispering into the ear of a paramour, if I don't have Love, it will be evident, and I'll be proven worthless. (v. 13)

If I have spiritual knowledge and any spiritual gift and can even know mysteries, if that knowledge is not covered in Love, then we must ask where is this so-called knowledge coming from? There is more than one individual that I've heard give what they call prophecy but it is cold and condemning and accusatory--, there is no Love in it. The Holy Spirit gives the Gift of Prophecy; the Holy Spirit is the Spirit of God. God is Love so why wouldn't anything and everything God says be covered in Love? Even when God sends a reproving Word there is still Love in it, every time. When a person comes off as harsh and condescending, I cannot listen to them, either right then, or further. The Spirit within me does not bear witness with the *spirit* that is in them.

It is not absolute that they are wrong, and I am right. It means that for now, this day, and for that *word* they are speaking, they are not called to me, and I am not called to them. The Lord will judge anything more.

If I have a faith that can move mountains, but do not have Love, then it seems that my faith is in *myself* and not in Love or for Love. Faith must be in God. Without Love, no matter what I do it will be for myself, to glorify myself then what others gain may be fleeting, but I will actually gain nothing with the wrong desire to do a thing.

Love is the greatest, but it is also a lot of work. But are we not commanded to love one another? Love is work because the flesh must be suppressed in order for Love to thrive and grow. All works of the flesh are **anti-Love**. Some of you already know how hard it can be to overpower your flesh and bring it under the auspices of the Holy Spirit.

Now let's turn to the most beautiful book on love in the Bible--, probably in the whole world, the Song of Solomon.

Agape is the **Love** that you don't have to ask a person if they love you; if they *agape* you, **you know it**. <u>**God Agape**</u>

Loves us, and don't' we know it? The other kinds of love, not so much--, you usually have to ask. Still, you can be in love with your spouse and never doubt if they love you by the way they show their love toward you, by the way they treat you, dwelling with you according to knowledge. They've learned your Love language and honor it. The housewife doesn't have to ask for grocery money every week, does she? The husband doesn't have to ask for his meal to be cooked or served every night, does he? He doesn't have to ask why his clothes are not laundered, or picked up from the dry cleaners, does he? She doesn't have to wonder why her car is not serviced or washed, as these are things they do for one another as a point of care, honor, and love.

But when folks are demonstrating love by *works* and one is not doing loving things, or only doing the absolute minimum--, (breadcrumbing), the partner may have to ask, *Do you love me?* That is either a set up to the next thing they will ask, or it is an innocent question because the one asking feels a deficit in some way between the two of them in their relationship.

I sincerely believe that when you *agape* someone there is no question whatsoever as if you love them or not. And if they *agape* you--, you will know it undeniably.

Agape Love is the greatest Love, but it still can break your heart. It must because of the power in it, and because of the magnitude of Love.

Shulamite Woman

This is the story of a Shulamite woman. Shulamite comes from the word, *sheloma*, which means peaceful and may be the feminine version of the word, the name, *Solomon*, so it is no coincidence that she is the woman in this Book of the Bible.

Tell me where is the one whom I so lovest.
Where thou feedest where thou makest
thy flock to rest at noon. And why should
I be as one that turned aside by the flocks
of thy companions?
(Song of Solomon 1:7)

The Shulamite woman had met herself a guy; she had met herself, a dude. She had met herself a man, and she thought he was something special. She thought that she loved this man. As a matter of fact, she decided that she loved him and desired intimacy with him. She desired to spend time with him. She even desired, the Word says, his kisses--, the kisses of his lips. She liked his pleasing perfume, his presence, and the sweetness of his name. She loved everything about him and she wanted to be wherever he was.

She wanted to go away with him and run after him. She had it bad. This Shulamite woman had even asked her girlfriends about him.

She said, *Don't you think he's fine? Don't you think he's altogether lovely don't you think he's all that?*

The Shulamite wanted to know from him, *Where do you feed your flocks? Where are you in the middle of the day? Where are you at noon?* She wants to know because she wants to go where he is.

Today, young people who think you've *met a guy* and he's *all that*, you want to know, *Where do you play basketball? Where do you hang out? What time will you be at the mall? Are you a gamer? Where are you gonna be? 'Cause I wanna be where you are.* And you don't really care who knows. Really, you want people to know that you're with him.

Single women I challenge you to correct your mistakes—because there are more than one. The first mistake is that we ask the man where he *plays* instead of where he **works**. Of course, we want to talk to him on his down time, but we need to make sure he works and is industrious *first*.

What time do you get off from work? That is the better question, women.

The Shulamite woman had the Wisdom to ask the man, Where you going to be *working* in the middle of the day? But the modern female wants to know, where you gonna be *hanging out* where you gonna be playing?

But she asked her girlfriends all the superficial questions such as, *Do you think he's good looking? Do you think he's fine? Do you know where he is? Don't you think he's all that?*

In the Song of Solomon, you'll see the daughters of Jerusalem had to agree with her because he was fine, he was all put together; he was *all that*. This man had it going on. Oh, glory to God --, well, at least in the natural; he was a real hunk.

She had asked him where was he gonna be? Where is he going to be **working**? The one that she loves tells her, Find out what I love and go there. He basically was saying, *I do a job that I love and what I love is where I will be.*

Well, in the Song of Solomon, this man was a shepherd. He loved the sheep so therefore she had to find out where the sheep were going to be to find out where he would be.

He is saying, *Learn me, know me, then you can be with me.* Take a lesson.

Fortunately, this man thinks she's lovely too. He wants to *dine* with her. He wants to sup with her, else she'd be pursuing him only and that is *masculine energy* that women should not put on because that would be a second mistake.

In the process of this would-be courtship, there are some angry brothers. Some don't want you following after the one that you love. Most brothers don't think that anybody is good enough for you anyway. I've got three brothers; I know something about that. One of my brothers ran my very first date away. The two of us were going to an afternoon matinee and he would bring me back by 7pm. My date came to pick me up too early, so I wasn't at home. However, my brother was there when my date came to take me to a movie.

Furthermore, family members or people who knew you first may be using you, or still using you to help them and do not want you to go and start and build your life with another. This is demonic and diabolical, but it is not new. The Word even says the Shulamite woman had helped her brothers dress their vineyards but had not attended to her own.

Oh, sister-saints of God, this is a third mistake to correct. Brother-saints—you too. Be good to your family of origin but there comes a time for you to leave and cleave to your own family.

In the Song of Solomon, though, this is a bona fide love affair because he thinks she's lovely. She thinks he's lovely. It's a bona fide, 2-sided love affair. Glory to God. This seems like the start of something really good.

The One You Love

Not everyone will be happy with the one you love; you've got to know that you know that you heard from the Lord regarding the one that you Love. In the case of the Shulamite woman, this is a bona fide love affair, not a one sided or lopsided, flop-sided love affair.

> Stay with me flagons comfort me with apples because I am sick of love…
> comfort me with apples for I am sick of love. (Song of Solomon 2:5)

Angry brothers or no, after a period of time, the Shulamite woman has indulged in this mutual love with the object of her affections so much that now she's love-sick. She's found the one that her soul loves and she's become *faint with love.*

She is lovesick but I warned you earlier that love **breaks your heart**. How can that be? When love is so good that you don't even want to eat, then love is really having an effect on you.

Yet, the story progresses. The love story progresses and the man in this love story Solomon tells her, *Come away with me.*

Come Away with Me

Arise and come away with me,
(Song 2:13)

The man asked her to come away with him, but the Shulamite woman didn't go. You see she was having a love hangover. She was basking in the glory of all this romance.

He had to go because he had something to do. The brother had business to take care of. He had work to do. He told her, The fig trees are putting forth green figs. The sycamore figs in that region bore figs four times a year, so this man was busy. The brother had something to do; this was another season in the man's life where he had to go. So, he went away.

Obviously, he's a man set under authority, and he had purpose, so he had to answer to somebody. Trust me, that's the kind of man you want, Singles. That's the kind of man you want.

He had to go, but he invited her. Again, that's the kind of man you want--, you want a man who is inclusive and will include you in his life, in his activities and sometimes in his trips that he takes, both business jaunts and leisure holidays. (Song of Solomon 3 1-7).

The man who is always using the words, *I* and *me* is not relational. He may not even be transactional, but at most he is transactional. The man who says *we* and *us* and is relationship-focused, he is a builder and is looking for a lasting connection.

I and *me* is most likely going to break your heart. *I* and *me* is the person that you will have to ask if they love you because something is missing in their deeds and words.

We and *us* is the keeper.

By Night

By night on my bed, I sought him whom
my soul loveth. I sought him but I found
him not. (Song 3:1)

My mother would quote Alfred
Lord Tennyson: *Tis better to have loved
and lost than never to have loved at all.*
However, that saying didn't seem to work
for the Shulamite woman.

Why didn't it work?

Because she in essence said in
Verse 2 of the Song of Solomon, *I'm
gonna get up now, I'm gonna rise now and
I'm going to go about the city, in the
streets and in the broad ways, and I'll seek
him whom my soul loveth.*

I sought him and I found him not.

The Shulamite woman got up and went after this man. Yes she did. She didn't care who knows and she came to Verse 3.

And the Watchmen that go about the city found me to whom I said saw him whom my soul loveth.

This woman had no shame. She asked the people, *have you seen him? Have you seen him tell me, have you seen him?*

It was but a little that I passed from them, but I found him whom my soul loveth: I held him, and would not let him go, until I had brought him into my mother's house, and into the chamber of her that conceived me.
(Song of Solomon 3:4)

She brought him into a place of intimacy. Even though *goes into* equals married, until you say, *I do* in the natural, you are not considered married. That is a **loophole** that a lot of flesh-minded people are counting on. They reason that since they didn't go to a preacher or a Justice of the Peace, even though they *went into,* they are not married. That is a technicality that can be used in the natural, but spiritually, goes into equals married. Better find out what God says about that. God says *goes into* equals married.

Anyway--, real intimacy requires *covenant*, it requires an agreement between two, or all who are in the covenant. I'm saying two since we are talking about a marriage-type covenant. If you are all into him but he's just into the act that you two are committing, that is not mutual *intimacy*. If you are all into her, but she's just having fun or passing the time, or proving that she can get you into bed, that is not mutual intimacy. There is no agreement; there is no covenant. Even if there is a marriage on paper and only one is honoring the covenants of marriage, are **both** even in the marriage? Is there real intimacy?

Behold his bed, which is Solomon's three score valiant men are about it, of the value of Israel the king. (v. 7)

A guard was set outside the private chambers of Solomon's intimate place. Don't we do some of the same things, ourselves? Locked doors, do not disturb signs, babysitters are called, kids are sent to grandma's or to a friend's house for a sleepover so there are no interruptions. At least we lock the bedroom doors—hey, that's kind of like setting a guard for privacy. After all, *Kingdom Business* should be going on between a man and a woman who are in a Godly marriage covenant.

Real Love

I've been to productions of the Song of Solomon, hailing the great love story of Solomon and the Shulamite woman. The man and the woman recite the different parts of this Book, and it is quite moving as a couple's ministry.

Yet, this is an image, a reflection of what a Love affair with Jesus should look like. Yes, it should be like, Kiss the son lest he be angry (Psalm 2); we need to get up close and personal with the Lord. We want intimacy from the Lord; when we want God's attention, we really want it--, and God wants intimacy with us. He also wants exclusivity; He's Jealous. He is a jealous God. He wants no idols or anybody before Him.

By night on our beds, we aren't thinking about anything else--, *are we*? We're thinking about Jesus. We're thinking about the One whom our soul loves and we go, or should go looking for Him. Oh, we go looking for Him all right, if something is going wrong in our natural lives. If something is not working the way we want it to be working, we seek God. If we or someone in our family is sick, or the money is funny we will chase after God.

Any of us will go looking for Jesus. We'll get up out of our beds, and we may pace from one end of the house to the other. We could pace a hole in the carpet, and wear the shine off the floor, marching and praying and praying, seeking the One whom your soul loves--. 'cause you love Him right then because you know He's the only one that can help you, Selah.

And Jesus turned and saw them following and said unto them, what seek ye?
(John 1:38-39)

They said into him, Rabbi, which is to say, being interpreted, *Master*, where dwelleth thou?

And He saith unto them, Come and see. They came and saw where He dwelt, and abode with Him that day, for it was about the 10th hour.

Come on, folks--, all the people that He fed and healed, and He spoke this doctrine that was so new and it was so powerful and so people wanted to know who is this man? Jesus had a reputation and a fame. He didn't come to Earth to make a reputation for Himself, but He ended up having reputation.

Where does He live? Is He the same as the rest of us, and if not how is He different? He had a paparazzi. A rabbi-razzi. They were looking for Him and they wanted to know where He lived, so they ended up going to Jesus' house.

Even now, the Lord invites you to come and be with Him. Not just to become casually acquainted with Him--, you could do that at church, but Jesus wants so much more. He wants to share **intimate** time with you. So, you, also, have got to

go to His *house* and spend some personal
and alone time with the Lord.

Invite Him Again

When you got saved you invited the Lord into your life. But it would still be appropriate to say, *Welcome* every day and not just ignore God or take Him for granted. Invite Him by worship into your days and nights to spend some personal time with the Lord. Worship Him in the beauty of His Holiness. Tell Him that He is lovely, and that He is worthy and that He's the Prince of Peace. This is worship. Say these things to His face, as it were. Simply because you are seeking His face, and you want the Lord's face turned toward you; that is favor. That is protection. That is relationship and intimacy.

In the natural, real intimacy usually begins with two looking into one another's eyes which they say are the windows of the soul.

The Lord says that when we are suddenly and desperately seeking Him, pacing the floor, wearing out the carpet and stripping the shine off the hardwood floors that we are most often asking Him to do something for us. When we're looking for the Lord, urgently wanting Him to help us, we are only seeking His hand. God is not against petition prayer, but God is more than just a provisional hand.

If I walk up to someone and proceed to talk to his hand, how weird is that? How rude is that? Isn't that what the kids say? Talk to the hand because the ears aren't listening.

Talking to His hand, I might as well say, *Hand, feed me, hand, give me. Hand bless me; you do such good things for me, oh hand.* When you talk to the hand you're saying. *I need money and I need food, and I need the bills paid, and I need, I need, I need, help me, help me, help me.*

What kind of love is this? What kind of love is it when you objectify the person you say you love and focus on the thing that they have, or things that you want from them, not acknowledging the whole person? Is that *Agape* Love?

No, that's the kind of "love" or affection that a man may give an idol, and when it is done to God, that surely must break His heart. Yes, God's heart can break too.

God is not telling us to talk to the hand because His ears are listening His ears are inclined to us. We seek after all of the Lord, not just His hand but we also seek His face as the psalmist says.

Lord, thy face I will seek, (Psalm 27)

You seek His face, because that's where the *intimacy* starts; that's where the *intimacy* is. That's where the relationship is. You are not going to have an intimate relationship with anybody's hand, or any

42

other body part, in the natural but with the whole person. And you look them right in their face; you look into their eyes.

When you are in the presence of someone that you love or someone you believe loves you, but they won't look at you, then you are offended, insulted and hurt. You pretty much think they hate you, don't you? Should God be different than that? We are created in His image and likeness, and He lives in a House just like we do. Doesn't God have feelings and emotions? We say we love God but we are neither looking for Him or towards Him unless we want something?

Not one of us can fool God. Don't break God's heart with *fake* love; His heart could be broken just because you tried to pull that stunt on Him, and now He's got to wait for your repentance, or He will have to deal with you.

I Found Him

Thankfully, we've found Jesus, and we've taken Him into our most intimate place--, into our heart, into our bedrooms, and into our prayer closets. We haven't let anyone stop us or hinder us. This is like setting a guard like Solomon set 60 soldiers outside of his intimate place--, 60 soldiers. Hmm...

We don't let anybody bother us until we spend quality time with the Lord--, especially when we need something. We are in Love. We've met Jesus, we've been born again. We are serious about this, *aren't we?*

But if we don't need anything, if we just want to love on Him, if we just want to talk to Him, sing to Him, praise Him, and listen for His words back to us, no one should disturb us. If we want to be intimate with Him, we also set a guard such as silencing the phone and going into a quiet place and a quiet time. *Right*?

If we are really serious, we've been fasting; maybe we haven't eaten. Hopefully it was a voluntary, dedicated fast and not just that we forgot to eat because we have super busy lives. Maybe we were pursuing after God, so busy being God chasers we haven't eaten anything. Some of us have been fasting for five years, trying to get into the presence of God. Some have become sticks and bones. That's about what we've become trying to get into the presence of God. Oh, He's worth it; that's how good He is. That's how sweet He is.

Just this week the Lord showed me His sweetness. It was just a quiet moment in prayer, and the Presence of the Lord came into the room and imparted a knowing and an understanding of how sweet He is.

Oh taste and see that the Lord is good. He is sweeter than the honey in a honeycomb. He's sweet, I know.

So, we've set a guard. Maybe you have turned on the music in your room, locked the door and told your spouse, "Get the kids out of here--, *I need some quiet time. Don't bother me.*" You might mute the telephone or go into the bathroom and lock yourself in there for a while. Perhaps some prayers and Godly meditation is what we do in the bathtub. We might be in the bubble bath praying.

It's all about our uninterrupted and intimate time with the Lord. My car is a solitary time with the Lord for me; God ministers to me there.

In Love With Jesus

We're so in love with Jesus, we got Jesus pins, and Jesus scarves. We got the Bibles with our names engraved on them. We are in love. We have met Jesus. We've been born again. We are wide open in love. Plus, we should be in relationship, and having *intimacy* with the Lord Jesus. Amen.

This is Jesus. We must give Him His *time*. Don't play, 'cause you know you give your loved ones in the natural their time and attention. God does way more for any of us than any human, so how can we put any human ahead of God? Plus, your friends and families have **what** Heaven or hell to put you in or save you from? Giving more to anyone than to God is idolatry, you know; and God hates idolatry.

If Solomon and the Shulamite woman were courting on the telephone today, she would have situated herself into whatever room in which she could speak freely and privately. They may have whispered and giggled and gushed into the phone to one another for hours at a time. Can you imagine it?

Hey *Solly.*

Hey *Shully. You fine.*

You know you handsome, Baby, I love you so much.

I love you too, Shully.

I Love your perfume. I love this. I love this, I love that about you. Love, love, love. Love, love, love.

C. S. Lewis wrote about the four kinds of love. He said the people who are in love talk to each other **about their love**. But people who are friends don't really talk very much about their friendship.

If you're not talking very much to the Lord, or not speaking to Him relationally, but you believe that you are saved, perhaps you are just friends with Him. If you're not talking to the Lord very much about your relationship or how wonderful He is, perhaps you two are only acquaintances and friends. Thank God for friendships, but you talk about your love, and you talk about the one that you love to that person and to whomever else will listen.

You can't stop talking about him or her. All of this Love opens you up, it opens up your emotions and it opens up your spirit and it makes you vulnerable, actually.

You're in love again and that changes everything. Love has just broken into your life and torn down all your walls. It has torn down all your self-made walls. It has torn down all the walls that the enemy has silently been building to block you off from God and to even barricade you against normal human relationships with other people. As long as you love and keep yourself open to Love you are far better off than if you don't. The main reason is that if you shut off Love, all kinds of evil *spirits* can get in and occupy your heart. If Love is on the throne of your heart, that means that God is ruling your heart and life. The Power of Love will run off a multitude of evil from every broaching your life or squatting there.

Thank God that Love has broken in, if it is real Love. Once in, you've just and automatically erased at least one, or some, or maybe and hopefully all your own rules that you've established to keep you alone and lonely in this world. You know those rules such as:

- *I'm never gonna do this again.*
- *I'm not gonna let that happen again.*
- *No, don't nobody call me.*
- *I'll never fall in love again.*
- *I'm never going to trust another guy again.*
- *I'm never going to do that again.*

You know all those rules with *never's* and *ever's* in them. If you look closely, every "rule" goes with a spirit, a work of the flesh: unforgiveness, bitterness, resentment, jealousy, division, and so on. Every one of the works of the flesh interferes with your relationships with real people. The devil's plan to divide and conquer should not be still working against you, so stop letting him trick you.

If you commit those works, buy into them, don't repent of them, they stay. You harbor them, they do their worst against you.

Now the works of the flesh are manifest, which are these; Adultery, fornication, uncleanness, lasciviousness, Idolatry, witchcraft, hatred, variance, emulations, wrath, strife, seditions, heresies, Envyings, murders, drunkenness, revellings, and such like: of the which I tell you before, as I have also told you in time past, that they which do such things shall not inherit the kingdom of God. (Galatians 5:19-21)

Until

Now you've met Jesus; you're born again, you're blessed, and you know it. Hallelujah; you're a new creation. You're made brand new. You can't praise Him enough. You can't go to church enough. You can't bless His name enough. You can't pray enough--, no amount of praying is too much. You can't do anything related to God enough. You're talking about Him all the time. Jesus this, and Jesus that--, you are wide open and in love.

You finally have found Him whom your soul loveth.

Until one day Jesus tells you something that you don't want to hear. He gives you something to do that you don't want to do. One day, Jesus says, *Arise and come away with Me.*

You say, *Where are we going?*

Jesus in an echo from the Song of Solomon may say, *The fig trees are putting out green figs and I gotta go.* Jesus wants to take you to the next level of your Christian walk, to the next place of relationship and intimacy. Jesus might want you to go out into the fields that are white to harvest to win souls.

It will take a proper relationship with Christ to do any good works because Christ will work through you. This is the purpose of your connection, covenant and intimacy with Christ, it is to do good works. It's for you too, but not just so you can feel good about yourself and make sure you're going to Heaven.

You can't just stay at home praying and reading the Bible all day, or only go to church to worship with the other saints. You are designed for good works and to win souls outside of the church and the four walls of your house.

But Jesus, you might say, *"I'm saved, I don't need to go anywhere.* Or worse, you may say, *I'm too saved to go anywhere."*

Surely, I'm not going to sin again 'cause I'm saved. But then you sin again in the middle of your salvation.

Thank God for Mercy. Thank God for the Blood of Jesus.

Thank God for confession and repentance. All of us have sinned and fallen short, and once you get saved, you can still sin. But thank God for the conviction of the Holy Spirit, and right relationship being restored back to the Father, Hallelujah.

Hard Questions

So, Jesus may tell you something you don't want to hear. He may tell you, *No*, when you want a *Yes*. He may tell you *Yes* when you want to hear a *No*. He may not say anything at all because He's already told you the answer 14 times before. Now He's either told you to stop asking or He has stopped repeating Himself. So, you ask again, and He is not talking, not saying anything at all, then all of a sudden, you're just sick of Love.

All this Love and all this Jesus stuff, you may lament.

Jesus may instruct you to do something you don't want to do.

*Jesus, I don't wanna do that. Be nice to some more of **those** people. Those church people--, be nice to them?*

Pray for those that despitefully use you.

Those people?

The Word says to love one another.

*Love **those** people? Lord, they hate me.*

Bless those that hate you.

Love those people? Love those people, you repeat, whining.

All of a sudden you just sit there, you're sick of church, you are sick of the church people, you're sick of the choir rehearsals. You're sick of this and sick of that. You are suddenly sick of Love.

This is a different kind of Love sickness because Love is breaking your heart. You may be ready to cop out and drop out, pop out, flop out. You may be ready to fall out. You are sick of Love; it's that simple.

So, you think.

Two-Way Love

What used to be a two-sided bona fide love affair with the Lord is at risk by your own disobedience. Now you are asking, *Jesus, why are you asking me to do that? I thought You loved me.*

And Jesus is saying, **I thought you loved Me. If you love Me**, He said, **You will keep My commandments.**

But you are sick of Love, and you said within yourself, *Hey it don't take all of that.* You have even asked your angry brothers who don't want you to be saved in the first place anyway. You go and ask them, but what you're really asking them is, *How is your life?*

You are asking them their opinion, wanting to know if their life is better than yours without telling them that Jesus just asked you to do something really hard that you don't want to do. Yet, you are wondering, is the grass really still green out there on the other side, which wasn't even green in the first place, or you wouldn't have come into the Kingdom seeking Salvation.

Some of you ran into the church because you finally came to the realization that you are not cut out for the world. The world had chewed you up, and spit you out because you can't handle the world but there you are trying to be both in it and *of* it..

Finally, you came to a place where you belong, fell in love with Jesus. And now, since Jesus has asked you to do something hard, suddenly, you are sick of Love.

So, in essence, you ask angry brothers who didn't want you saved in the first place, *Is your life better?*

Jesus asked you the hard questions or He gave you a difficult instruction, or a seemingly impossible assignment, so you think. So, you either have not answered it or you've answered it in the negative and now think you've gotten off the hook with the assignment.

But Jesus is saying to you, *I thought you wanted to be where I was. I thought you wanted to be with Me. I thought you wanted to do what I do.*

Oh, He said, *Wait a minute I thought we were in love. I thought we had a connection. I thought we had Covenant. I thought I could talk to you straight.* He says, *Aren't you supposed to be planning to be part of my Bride?*

The Church is to be the Bride of Christ. I'm not marrying a child, and right now, you are acting childish, you gotta grow. You gotta grow up. I thought you were mature, or maturing, I thought you could take the Truth.

I gotta take the Truth? You ask yourself, out loud.

Oh, Love breaks your heart.

Jesus says, *If you Love Me you keep My commands. If you Love Me you do my will. If you Love Me you do as I would do. If you Love Me you show compassion. If you Love Me--, you said you Love Me.*

Well, I do Love You Lord, but--, but what you've asked me to do--, and there you are steadily saying, *I do* with your mouth. But your actions are saying, **I don't.**

Where is the intimacy? Your mouth is saying *I do*. As said earlier, until you **say** *I do,* you don't have intimacy because you don't have agreement or covenant. But you're saying *I do* with your mouth but with your body and your actions you are saying *I don't*, when you say, *I won't.*

Where is the intimacy? You don't have the intimacy until you say *I do*, and then you **do** what *I do* says you do.

Sick of Love

The Shulamite woman was all into this love affair at the beginning but then all of a sudden in Chapter 5, she's sick of love. She's had too much but in a different way than one person bowing out of a relationship.

The Shulamite was still pursuing; she went through the streets looking for that man, but guards had beat her up while she was out there. She is sick of love. Depending on your temperament and purposes in a relationship, Love can make you love sick; Love breaks your heart.

I charge you daughters of Jerusalem if you
find my beloved that you tell him that I'm
sick of love, (Song of Solomon 5:8)

Love Breaks Your Heart

There was a great prophet named Ezekiel. I want to tell you about his heart for just a minute.

Say to the House of Israel. This is what the sovereign Lord says, I'm about to desecrate my sanctuary. The stronghold in which you take pride, that delight of your eyes, the object of your affection, the sons and daughters who left behind, will fall by the sword, and you will do as I have done. You will not cover the lower part of your face or eat the customary food of mourners. You will keep your turbans on your heads, in your sandals, on your feet. You will not mourn or weep, but will waste away because of your sins and groan among yourselves. Ezekiel will be a sign to you and you will do just as he has done. When this happens, you will know that I am the sovereign Lord. (Ezekiel 24:21-24 NIV).

Here's Ezekiel, *son of man*, minding his own business. He was doing nothing but what the Lord was telling him to do. He's prophesying. He's been obedient; he has seen great visions. And God has just told him that the light of his eyes, the object of his affection, is going to be lost to him. This is his wife. That's bad enough, but he also says he will also lose his sons and his daughters.

After all of this loss, the Word of the Lord says **Ezekiel cannot mourn**. He cannot mourn this loss. He must go on business as usual.

Love breaks your heart. Sometimes Jesus will tell you to do something you don't want to do. He'll tell you something to do that you just don't feel that there's any strength in you or certainly there's no real desire to do it. Love breaks your heart. Yet, there things you do because of Love because you love the Lord. And these things are in and further the great plan of God for mankind; there is Purpose and Destiny in everything God does and instructs us to do.

Ezekiel may be saying, *But Lord, I Love You, I Love You. I've sought intimacy with You, I have spent time with You in the night hours. I have been a watchman on the wall. On my bed I've sought You. I sought You first thing in the mornings, and I guarded our intimate time together. I opened myself up to You, and so doing You gave me the desires of my heart. You gave me the delight of my eyes. You gave me the object of my affections. Lord, I thank You and I praise You for it.*

So, Lord, what's going on?

Love breaks your heart. Sometimes the Lord will ask you to do hard things, even heart-breaking things. He especially did of His prophets. So, anyone who would seek to be a prophet when that is not their calling is not wise at all. Ezekiel's heart will be broken, albeit with advanced notice, but it will be broken. Further, he cannot mourn, but he must go as if his heart was not even broken.

My lover is to be a sachet of myrrh resting
between my breasts,
(Song of Solomon 1:13; NIV).

Myrrh was an embalming spice. It's a symbol of Jesus' death and His Cross. The smell of myrrh even in the beginning of the Song of Solomon overwhelmed the Shulamite, even more than the other fragrances and aromas that she was speaking of.

Myrrh speaks of suffering. In life and in love, there will be some suffering. **Love breaks your heart.** Intimacy, relationship, and even covenant marriage--, for better or for worse, may break your heart. After you've let Love break into your heart, Love now breaks your heart. This was explained at the beginning of this book, due to the shear Power of Love and the magnitude of it, the heart will break.

The Lord may be asking as you are asked the hard questions, or asked to do the hard things, as He asked Ezekiel, **Don't you Love Me?**

Ezekiel by his obedience answers, *Yes, Lord, I do.*

If you Love Me, you will keep My commandments. I you Love Me, you'll minister My Word, you will minister to My sheep.

Ezekiel may be insisting, *Lord, why must I do this?*

Because you Love Me.

You obey because you love God, but what's in it for me? Ezekiel may be wondering.

And the Lord says, I have set this example Ezekiel; you're the example.

Do as he does--, as God says. Verse 24 *Ezekiel will be a sign to you and you will do just as he is done. When this happens you will know that I am the sovereign Lord.*

The welfare of all of Israel depends on this example that this prophet, this man Ezekiel sets before them.

I Love you Ezekiel and I Love everyone in Israel. I Love the world. I love them so much that I'm going to send them Love in a few hundred years. But for now, this is a temporal thing, Ezekiel with eternal ramifications.

Thou lovest Me before the foundation of the world. (John 17:24)

Ezekiel had to have realized that before he was formed in his mother's womb, the Lord knew him. And he had to have known that the Lord loved him, even then.

So, Ezekiel obeyed God.

Who did it save? Who did it deliver? Who got well? Who got financially blessed? Who got a new house? Nobody. But Ezekiel Loved the Lord, and he did what he was told. The ways and the thoughts of the Lord are far higher than ours. There is purpose and destiny and Love in everything God does and instructs us to do.

Saints, if Ezekiel, by this time, was sick of Love after that incident, we don't know about it. It's not really mentioned in the Scriptures. But he suffered for the sake of obedience, for the sake of the Word of the Lord, for the sake of the people, and for the sake of his purpose and prophetic calling, and for the sake of Love.

Before the Foundation

God sent another man to Earth. For God so Loved the world that He sent His Only Begotten Son. The Love that God has for us, He put in the vessel, in the package, in the man called Jesus. And God, before the foundations of the world had told Jesus what to do, and Jesus had done it before the Earth and World were formed.

The lamb was slain before the foundation of the world.
(Revelations 13:8)

Worthy is the lamb that was slain to receive power and riches and wisdom and strength and honor and glory and blessing. (Revelations 5:12)

But God, like Abraham, had taken His Son up to a high place, overlooking the city. Abraham took Isaac up to Mount Moriah, laid down the wood and secured his son to the altar in preparation to sacrifice him. Although that surely had to break Abraham's heart--, even the process of it, Abraham did not have to sacrifice his son after all.

But God. God allowed Jesus to be brought up to Calvary and He was secured to the altar, that Cross. But God sacrificed His Son, and that surely broke God's heart.

Love breaks your heart. Love even breaks the heart of God.

Jesus had come to Earth with His heart full of Love for the world. The Love that the Father loved Jesus with was in Him, *for us.* Jesus had Love for the whole world. Even the soldiers that beat Him and pressed that crown of thorns onto His head --, He loved them anyway.

The Shulamite woman was beaten in the streets as well. The love she had for Solomon was <u>not</u> the *Agape Love* necessarily, so she wasn't a representation of the ultra-forgiving God kind of Love. It is simply not stated in that passage how she felt towards these brutal watchmen in the streets.

But Jesus said, **Father, forgive them for they know not what they do.**

For God so Loved the world that He had sent Jesus, and that same Love God had put in Jesus, *for us.* The *agape* Love of God was put in Jesus Christ.

Saints of God, *eros, erotic "love"* will not be in Heaven; men and women will not be given to marriage there. And, of course in the Heavens, they will not burn in lust for one another, either.

To really, truly Love someone unconditionally is a gift of God. It is not something we know innately. It is not something we can even understand with our human minds. It could be modeled before us and we can receive the example of it; but not always, and some do not receive ever the *agape* that God sends them. It's as though they have no Love receptors on the inside of them. God is Love and Jesus is Love and the Holy Spirit is the Spirit of God, so **He is also Love**. If there is no Spirit within a person to receive the Love of God, it won't land. And, cannot be forced upon a person.

If you've ever been in love with someone--, and you love them with the purest of Loves, but they don't receive it. Or worse, if they reject you and the Love you offer, they haven't rejected you, they've rejected God. Know that, and be at peace with yourself.

Agape Love is a gift of God. To love someone unconditionally is a choice you make. You choose to love them as Christ would Love them. What? What if they have no Love receptors inside of themselves. They may have lust and sex receptors and may play along with you for a while to see what they can get out of it, but if they may not be able to understand or receive real Love. That's a real possibility if they have a hardened, stony heart. You love them the way and as long as God says. After that, you may part company with them and shake the dust.

So, Jesus comes to Earth with all of this Love for us, and His heart is wide open. You know your heart is wide open when you are *in love*. And you really feel it because when somebody mistreats you a little bit, you act up. You may exclaim, *You shouldn't have done this. I'm gonna run away, and I'm not going to speak to him anymore. I'm not taking all of this. It don't take all of that. I was not made for this. I'm not putting up with it.*

It hurts so much because your heart was wide open, you were especially vulnerable because you cared for them. Even the Word says, It wasn't a stranger that did this to me, it was someone that I knew. It was someone that I trusted somebody that I cared about. The closer a person is to you, if they betray you, the more it seems to make your heart ache. And that's what makes your heart break.

Love breaks your heart.

If you don't care about the person what they do to you won't really bother you that much. It may bother you a little bit, or for a little while, but not for long.

Was Jesus Sick of Love?

Love covers a multitude of sins, but in the Garden of Gethsemane, Jesus was sweating like blood. Was He sick of Love? I don't know. What you do or don't do because of Love will sometimes break your heart, even if you are being obedient. Even if you are doing exactly what God said to do **your heart can still be broken**.

Good or bad, no matter what kind of Love--, Love breaks your heart. It's what you do with that breakage and how you handle yourself that matters next in your walk with the Lord. It is how and if you let the Lord minister to you after a broken heart that matters most.

Remember that before the foundation of the world the Lord already knew you. Before you were formed in your mother's womb, the Lord knew you. The Lord Loved you then and He Loves you now. He has plans for you, plans for a future and an expected end. Therefore, everything He asks you to do, assigns to you, or tells you to do has both purpose and Love in it.

He loves you.

Covering the Multitude

Love covers a multitude of sins. That means that the Love that you have for the Father, the Love that you have for God will keep you from doing a multitude of things, a multitude of sins that you might do if you didn't have that Love.

Some say that it means that you cover up the shortcomings of others, that is you don't expose them and their misdeeds. I don't necessarily agree with that because then you become an enabler. And if you don't call out sin, that makes you complicit and a co-sinner in some cases. Covering implies darkness--, God says that what we forgive is forgiven and what we don't forgive remains. Covering the sin doesn't fit in that scenario for this writer. We don't put the sins of others on blast, after all, we all are sinners, but we speak the truth in Love, even to power. God's kingdom is one of Light, not of darkness.

This means that what you would do, because of Love, you won't even do it. Love constrains you, but Love also restrains you, and it motivates you. Love will make you do right. It'll make you do right. If you see Al Green, you tell him, that I said, *Love will make you do right. It will make you do right.*

And he went a little further and fell on his face and prayed saying Oh my father. If it be possible. Let this cup pass from me. Nevertheless, not as I will, but as thou wilt. (Matthew 26:39)

Do You Love Me, the Father asks?

He, Jesus went away again the second time and prayed saying, Oh my father, if this cup may not pass from me except I drink it. Thy will be done. (Matthew 26:42)

And the question--, the unspoken question remains, *Do You love Me?*

Jesus' consent came when He said, *Not my will, but thine, is the same as, I will go to the Mountain of Myrrh, I will go to Golgotha. I'll go to Calvary.*

Jesus is saying, *Yes* to the Cross. He consented because of Love. That's a Cross, people. That is death by crucifixion. That is a slow and painful death of the worst and most excruciating kind.

Love breaks your heart.

Love breaks your heart and the love that God loved Jesus with, this Love the very same Love that broke Jesus' heart is the same Love that sent Him to the Cross. Jesus ached for every one of us. His heart ached, no doubt and even His physical body ached--, for every one of us.

Love takes no less than everything. Love aches for everyone. Jesus' Love ached for every one of us. Jesus bled for every one of us. He took the beatings and opened *not* his mouth.

It was for every one of us. He
Loved and Loves every one of us. He
allowed His heart to be broken for every
one of us. He endured the Cross, the pain,
the shame, the humiliation for every one
of us.

Love, no doubt, broke His heart.

Not only that, Jesus **stayed** on the
Cross even though He could have called
more than 12 Legions of angels, that's
more than 72,000 angels. But He didn't;
He stayed the course and kept His word to
the Father even though His heart had to
have been broken.

We may not have authority over
that many angels, but sometimes we stay
in situations that we are placed in in life
because God said so. Love said so. Love
constrains and restrains us. We do it
because of Love. Only a person with a
heart *of flesh* could acquiesce to Love.
And, to receive that much love, maybe the
vessel has to be broken first.

But His Heart

The weight of all that sin was pinned to the Cross and dragged into hell, for every one of us.

Love takes no less than everything. Jesus gave it all. Jesus paid it all.

Now behold, the lamb, the precious Lamb of God born into sin that I may live again. The precious Lamb of God.

So, Jesus endured the Cross.

Not a bone on Him was broken, as was prophesied; this proves that He did not put up a fight; He surrendered. Even though He was beaten, had He put up opposition, His bones may have been broken.

Our bones form the structure to maintain our body. Jesus' prophetic destiny is to be married to the Body of Christ. His foundation is sound, it must be to support a Bride. His foundation was intact, hence not a broken bone. He was sin free; He had broken no spiritual laws so there was no iniquity. His foundation was secure. Let's face it, He's the Perfect Bridegroom.

But His heart.

He was a prime example of the *shalom* of God; nothing was missing and no bones on Him were broken. Therefore, there was no reason for Him to die and no reason that any man could put Him to death.

But His heart. No doubt, Love broke Jesus' heart.

When Ezekiel was about to lose his wife and his sons but could not mourn, but instead go on business-as-usual, God was showing us that when His Church (His Bride) is lost, **God** also has to carry on business as usual. When the sons that

He has raised up or desired to raise up fall or fail, God has to go on business as usual, even with a broken heart. All the times that it repented God that He had made man, He had to deal with that, but go on. Forward progress is the only choice we have in this life, saints of God.

LOVE breaks your heart.

A man with a broken heart hanging on a Cross, asking for forgiveness for those who broke His heart; how many of us could do that?

The Power

Love breaks your heart; it takes no less than everything. But, Love also breaks the chains and brings deliverance. Love is a Power, it is the Power of God and it is the Spirit of Deliverance. God so loves us that He wants us free, to be set free, and to freely Love Him. Jesus took captivity captive and made a spectacle of the devil.

Love aches for everyone.

Jesus on the Mountain of Myrrh was suffering because of Love and for the sake of Love. Love takes the suffering, and the pain, and love covers a multitude of sins. Love suffers long. Love forebears.

Love does not insist on its own way. Love
is the summation of the Fruit of the Spirit.

Set me like a seal upon your heart, like a
seal upon your arm. For love is as strong
as death. Jealousy is hard and cruel is
Shoal, which is the place of the dead. It
flashes are flashes of fire, most
vehement flame, the very flame of the
Lord. (Song 8:6~7)

Love Never Dies

Love never dies.

Lust dies; erotic love dies. It usually dies in about two years, if it even lasts that long. However, that is enough time to marry the wrong person and have one or more children before realizing that strong attraction was not Love at all.

Love is as strong as death. When something is as strong as something else, you can't conquer it or take it over. When we lose what we love or lose what or who we *think* we love, we grieve, whether they're dead or not. They could just be gone from a relationship. But it's still as if they died.

Jesus died spiritually when the Father turned His back on Him. All that sin that He carried to the Cross for us, killed Him spiritually. Without the Spirit of God in us, none of us are spiritually alive; instead, we are spiritually dead.

For if you sin, you shall surely die.
(Genesis 2:17)

Sin kills. The wages of sin is death. Jesus was already *spiritually* dead when He was nailed to that Cross. A major difference with Jesus, who could feel things spiritually such as virtue leaving Him, is that Jesus could, no doubt **feel** that He was spiritually dead. Where any of us could be walking around the planet with no idea that we are among the walking dead---, the spiritually dead, that is. The moment Jesus took on, least of all any sin and most of all, all that sin, He became spiritually dead.

Then His is body died after He gave up the Ghost.

After we sin and we are also spiritually dead, the devil can do with man as he pleases – easily nailing him to a cross or putting him in stockades to be humiliated and mocked. He can put man in yokes and bondages to make his life full of repeated hardships.

Yeshua gives us His Spirit and also gives us life to animate and empower us to fight the devil. In Him we move and breathe and have our being; as long as we are *in Him*. But if we are spiritually dead, we are no longer *in Him*. We've got to repent quickly and thoroughly and get back *in*.

If we yield to temptation, to sin and to the devil, our fight is diminished and sometimes entirely gone. This doesn't happen at once, else might we not feel it and know it, and do something about it? No, it can happen very slowly, nearly undetectably. Sometimes it happens over weeks, months, and years while people live defeated lives not knowing why things aren't going better than they are.

You sinned. You didn't repent and then you, like a malefactor got nailed to a demonic, invisible "cross" (in the spirit) for further torture, humiliation and ultimate death. Household witches and evil human agents helped the devil accomplish these demonic feats against you.

But if you believe on Christ and repent, today you can come down off that demonic cross if you ask the Lord. You can break out of bondages and be delivered back into the abundant life that Jesus came here and died for you to have. One on the Cross by Jesus did repent, and he was forgiven. The other's heart was hardened, he obviously saw hell.

God loves us so much that He would turn His back on a Perfect Man to make substitution for us. There was no Jewish Law to put a sin free man to death. Therefore, no one took Jesus' life; He laid it down. No one could take His life. But He had said in Scriptures that He had been given the power to lay down His life and take it up again.

Now we don't use Grace as an opportunity to sin, but by true, contrite repentance we invoke the power to take up our lives again, even if we have died due to sin in the past.

Lord, thank You.

Jesus said to His Father, *For thou lovest Me before the foundation of the world.*

The Father's Heart

Love breaks your heart.

God may be wondering, *Oh Man. O, sons of men, why are you like this? And why do I love you anyway?*

Ask anyone who has **truly** loved anyone, especially their child.

Don't you think it hurt the Father's heart to sacrifice His Only Begotten Son? Jesus Christ was a once and for all sacrifice.

We do not sacrifice our children. Folks, even getting pregnant on purpose and having a child that you don't even want; in order to get a relationship or some other perk is sacrificing the child. When a parent steals the child's life to live off the child at the child's expense, especially without the child's knowledge, that is also sacrificing the child. We do not sacrifice children. Ther is no Love in the sacrifice of children; it is a Herodian spirit and it honors the evil gods, Molech and Chemosh.

Jesus knew before the foundation of the world what His assignment was and why. It was for us--, for all of us. Jesus had agreed to it. He did it because of Love. In Gethsemane, Jesus knew that the death was His Father turning His back on Him. **Spiritual death was the death**. Jesus was not sweating like blood over the death of His physical body because He knew it would be raised up again. He didn't fear that which would kill the body and are not able to kill the soul.

Jesus said, Rather fear him, which is able to destroy both the soul and the body in hell.
(Matthew 10:28)

Jesus had lived a consecrated life. He was a man who knew no sin. So, He had no idea what it was like, or would be like to have no communion, no relationship, no intimacy with God. Jesus knew no sin; He *became* sin. He knew no death. He knew nothing about being out of relationship with the One He loved, but He went to the Cross because of the very Love He was to do without.

Love breaks your heart.

Walking Around the City

Set me like a seal upon your heart, like a
seal upon your arm. For love is as strong
as death. Jealousy is hard and cruel is
Shoal, which is the place of the dead. It
flashes are flashes of fire, most
vehement flame, the very flame of the
Lord. (Song 8:6-7)

Jesus loved the Father and us so
much and because of the Love that the
Father put in Him, that Jesus got up from
death. He got up from the grave. Jesus
went to hell, and there He may have said
something like, *Where's the one I Love?*
Where is the one I Love? Where are the
ones *that I Love?*

By night on my bed I sought him whom
my soul loveth: I sought him, but I
found him not.

I will rise now, and go about the city in
the streets, and in the broad ways I will
seek him whom my soul loveth: I sought
him, but I found him not.
(Song of Solomon 3:1-2))

When you love someone you look
for them. You want to be with them, you
want to find them. You check your phone-
-, have they called or texted? Can you find
him?

If you are believing for the
salvation of a loved one, you need to find
them, and don't let them go. Pray for them,
fast for them; never give up on them.

What did the Shulamite woman
do? She got up and went looking for the
one she loved.

When you Love it causes you to do
things. Love motivates you. Love inspires
you. Love empowers you. Love
strengthens your resolve; it fortifies you.

She got up.

She went looking for the one that her soul loved. She wasn't dead, so she didn't need to be resurrected to go looking for him, but she did need to get up and out, even in the night hours to find her beloved.

Resurrection power is that same power that got Jesus up out of the grave. Jesus started walking around the streets of the city--, **in Hell.** He started walking around in the city looking for the one He loved, looking for the ones that He loved. While He was down there in hell, looking--, He had you on His mind, He had me on His mind, even in Hell.

Most of us would have been just thinking of ourselves as we saw and or felt the fires, the smells, the torments in hell. Fear may have seized us; but Jesus did not have the *spirit of fear*, but one of Love, Power, and a sound mind. That is the Holy Spirit of God.

Saints, when you Love, really Love, you put that person at least on par with yourself or even ahead of yourself and you will care about them, think about them and seek to know of their wellbeing, sometimes over your own. Ask anyone who has a child. *Where is the one I love? Where is my beloved?*

I'm sure Jesus saw some horrors in hell, but He also saw some other things while He was walking through the streets of the city--, of Hell.

He took captivity captive, and He gave gifts unto men. If Jesus took captivity captive, that means **there was warfare in hell.** Surely, we know that a war broke out in Heaven and the devil was cast out, but have we not noticed that if Jesus took things from hell that belonged to God's people, then **warfare** was involved. I didn't say a battle, I said warfare. Sometimes warfare is just a spoken word.

Can the captive be taken away from the mighty? Can the lawful captive even be freed from the enemy? Yes. According to the Word and the power of God: Yes.

Jesus found Peace hidden away down there in hell. He may have said something like, *Devil, you don't know anything about Peace. You don't have any Peace with you. The stuff that you give people a drink and a smoke and--the false Peace that you give them--, that's not real Peace.*

You can't have their Peace; I'm taking this back and giving it to the ones that I love. Give Me that, I'm gonna give that to My beloved. You are His beloved. He wants to give you Peace, even Peace like a river.

And while He was walking around the streets, Jesus found joy. He may have said, *Devil this is not yours; you give Me this.* He also found health and healing down there, and He says, *I know some people who can use this; give that to Me.* So, He took it.

He found prosperity down there, saying, *This is for My people*, and He took that, and He gave gifts unto men. Jesus went to war and brought back spoils for the ones that He loves. Even in hell, even in warfare, on enemy turf, He had you on His mind. Surely someone may think of us and bring us a souvenir from a relaxing vacation; but hell was and is not a relaxing vacation; it is war and war is hell.

King of Glory

Can you imagine Jesus standing at the Gates of Hell commanding the Gates to lift up? **The King of Glory is coming in.**

Wait! What?

The gatekeepers of hell didn't expect that, did they? Jesus went into hell in full authority, in full power. *Lift up your heads O ye gates and be ye ever lift up.*

This could explain why the gatekeepers were talking back, saying, *"Who is this King of Glory?"* They'd never seen such a thing before. They were probably used to unrepentant sinners being dropped kicked, or kicking and screaming, moaning and crying helplessly into hell. Oh, but not Jesus; this was different. This was a different kind of Man---, this was an **innocent** man.

LIFT UP YE HEADS OH YE GATES. I AM COMING IN. And, I am coming in with Purpose, protection, on assignment and for victory. This guy wasn't coming in as a prisoner; He was coming in full authority. And, if He could command the gates to open for Him to come in, then He can also command the gates to STAY open and remain open so He can leave as He chooses.

GLORY TO GOD!!!

Jesus didn't go to hell as a Lovesick pushover. The devil probably thought that was Who he had crucified, but you can't kill Love. Love never dies. Love is a power; Love is the greatest Power.

Jesus went as the King of Glory. The Lord is a warrior; the Lord is His name.

His mission, even in hell may have been to find you, me, us, and any of our ancestors. *Where is My beloved? Where is the one that I love?*

Souls sentenced to hell with no way out, will not have to endure that sentence again if they accept Christ before death, even if it is the last minute. Just as did the malefactor beside Him on the Cross. No one said that man on the Cross was innocent Jesus was the only innocent one between the other two, but one took the *substitution* and went on to Paradise, even though he had to die for his sins against God, and crimes against man.

Jesus loves us with the Love of the Father. He will never, ever let us go. No one can take you out of His hands. Even if you find yourself on a cross and it is the very last minute. Don't wait until then, but don't not accept Jesus, even if it is the last thing you ever do on this Earth.

Even if while you are still alive you realize that you are in bondage, caught up in repetitive sin, in the devil's yoke, in a padlock, chains, ropes, ties--, in captivity, do not accept that. While you are still alive, call on Jesus to command the prison doors, the gates, the bars and anything that imprisons or holds you to let you go. Deliverance is for you. Call on the Lord, anytime day or night; He never slumbers nor sleeps. Amen.

Folks, when you've got something to do you get up from slumber, from sleep, from rest. Jesus had something to do. **Jesus had to go sit at the Right Hand of Glory.** There was no way He was going to stay in that grave.

Jesus also had to go get married because the Church is to be the Bride of Christ. He has to get married. How would it look on Jesus' wedding day as the Bride is adorned, looking good without spot, blemish or wrinkle and everybody's looking around asking, *Where's the bridegroom?*

Oh, He's still in hell.

No, I don't think so. He got up from there because He had something to do. Saints, in the natural if you're not married and want to be, and you should want to be--, get yourself out of hell. Get up out of the hell you've either created here on Earth or that you've allowed to encompass you so you can get a spouse, a helpmeet, and experience the good thing, obtain the favor of the Lord, and be fruitful and multiply, in the Name of Jesus.

Jesus had to get out of hell so He too can get married to the Church. You also need to get out of hell. Do it now while there is time.

And, you've got things to do now and in the afterlife. Your goal is to be married to the Lamb of God. That's why you want that intimacy—not sexual intimacy, but every other kind of intimacy, getting to know the Lord. That's how you relate to someone that you want to be married to.

Find Him

When you find your purpose, you're gonna get up from doing nothing or just waiting or watching time go by. If you're saved, you must know that Resurrection Power is still working in the Earth. It is still working in you. You were dead in sin and trespasses and the Resurrection Power of Christ brought you back to life when you accepted Christ. This power can resurrect your dead hopes. It can resurrect your dead dreams. It can resurrect the stuff that you thought was dead, and bring it back to life.

There is power in your calling and there's power in your purpose and there is power in your star; there is Power in working toward your destiny. Love is the greatest Power of all. God gives us Love and Love is not just a feeling or an idea, or an attitude; Love is a Power. Love is not just a spirit like the *spirits* that rule over the works of the flesh; LOVE IS A POWER. It is the greatest Power. With Love it should be easy to overcome the works of the flesh.

When you Love someone; you are giving them power. When someone loves you they are giving you Power. This is nothing to be played with. When it is mutual, you two really become a Power Couple. When it is one-sided it is so dangerous for the one doing all the giving.

Love **powers** the Gifts of the Spirit.

Why wouldn't God give you the greatest of powers to accomplish your purpose? *Agape Love* is THE Power over all the other powers and over the other kinds of love. You can do anything, all things through Christ and through the Love of God that strengthens you.

God sent us Love and He sent it by Jesus Christ.

What about you? Hasn't the Lord sent you to love some folks? Has He sent you to give them some Love?

It's not impossible. You can do this. You can do it even if it's people that are unlovely and you don't want to love them. Obey God; Love them anyway.

> But if a man would offer all the goods of his house for love, it would be utterly scorned and despised that as it wouldn't be enough.
> (Song of Solomon 8:7b AMP)

Money can't buy Love, not the real kind, not the *agape* kind. You can by some physical, flesh "love." But it cannot buy Love. Not only are the currencies incongruent, but there is also not enough money to buy Love. God cannot be bought.

Real Love, the big grown-up kind of Love, pure *agape* Love, it breaks your heart, your stony heart. But the good news is that God binds up broken hearts and he replaces stony, hardened hearts with a heart of flesh--, if you let Him. Ask Him.

King David was loved so much by God because his heart was after the heart of God. Love breaks your heart; not only can it, but it **must**. David experienced plenty of heartache and heartbreak in his life and if God was approving of David's heart, then surely it had been restored and remade into a heart of flesh that God approves of.

But first that human heart had to be broken – as does yours and mine.

A regular heart **must** be broken so that God can give you a heart of flesh. He gives you a heart that can contain real Love. He gives you a heart toward God, a heart for doing the things that God finds important. Find out who God loves, and go where those people are. Go where the people are that God loves. Go to the fields that are white to harvest. That's the kind of Love that is what real Love does.

Love is as strong as death. The intensity of true Love is so great but when it's lost, a person may feel as if someone has died. But usually by the time Love has broken your heart, **you are the person who has died**. Not a physical death, but your flesh has either died, or you've put it down willingly. **You have died because of Love**. Like Jesus you can be resurrected, today, tomorrow, over and again, as long as there is life. Repent. Renounce and denounce sin and all evil associations. Ask God to remove all iniquity, and be delivered. Arise and live!

Death is the last power that man has to oppose, and one of the surest weapons to defeat death is Love. Saints of God, **one may die many times as he lives.** That is the pain that we feel in life; it is the many deaths that we fight and refuse to allow. When we refuse to let something go. When we refuse to let something die because it pleases our flesh to keep it alive--, to keep it going.

Instead, if we were wiser, we would let it die so our hearts can grow and expand voluntarily so it won't have to break, or be broken into, or broken and hurt. Life is dynamic. We are going to change and grow as long as we are alive; no matter what. So, we might as well give in to it. We might as well give in to life and to Love. We yield to God and grow spiritually.

Conversely, we can fight Love and lose. God is Love and He is the greatest Power; He will always win--, even against YOU.

> For whosoever will save his life shall lose it: and whosoever will lose his life for my sake shall find it.

> For what is a man profited, if he shall gain the whole world, and lose his own soul? or what shall a man give in exchange for his soul?
> (Matthew 16:25-26)

King David, with a heart after God's own heart had many losses and heartbreaks, but he got up every time as well. The Shulamite woman got up because of love. Ezekiel had a broken heart, but could not even mourn, because of Love. Jesus got up, because of Love. Jesus is looking for you, shouldn't you also be looking for Him? You too--, won't you also get up, even from a broken heart, because of Love?

Jesus is looking for you; won't it be nice to finally be looking for someone who is looking for you, for a bona fide, 2-sided, mutual Love affair, instead of chasing shadows and maybes and people who don't even want to be found by you? Won't it be good to finally be found by someone who is offering you the real and right kind of Love?

Jesus is looking for you. He wants a two-sided, *bona fide* Love with **you**. Arise, and go through the streets until you locate Him, until you locate one another.

Many waters cannot quench Love. Neither can floods drown it.
(Song of Solomon 8:7a *emphasis added, mine*)

AMEN.

Dear Reader

Thank you for acquiring and reading this book. May Love find you. May you find Love. May you receive Love, willingly, without a fight, even if it breaks your heart. It's easier that way.

In the Name of Jesus,

Amen.

Dr. Marlene Miles

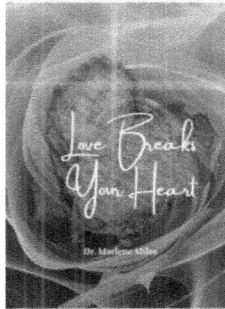

Prayer books by this author

While most books by this author have prayer points either throughout the book or at the end, there are some books that are **only** prayers. You just open up the book and pray. They are listed below:

Prayers Against Barrenness: *For Success in Business and Life*

Fruit of the Womb: *Prayers Against Barrenness*

Beauty Curses, *Warfare Prayers Against*
https://a.co/d/5Xlc2OM

Courts of Marriage: Prayers for Marriage in the Courts of Heaven
(prayerbook) https://a.co/d/cNAdgAq

Courtroom Warfare @ Midnight
(prayerbook) https://a.co/d/5fc7Qdp

Demonic Cobwebs *(prayerbook)*
https://a.co/d/fp9Oa2H

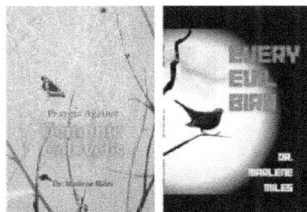

Every Evil Bird https://a.co/d/hF1kh1O

Every Evil Arrow
https://a.co/d/afgRkiA

Gates of Thanksgiving

Spirits of Death & the Grave, Pass Over Me and My House
https://a.co/d/dS4ewyr

Please note that my name is spelled incorrectly on amazon, but not on the book.

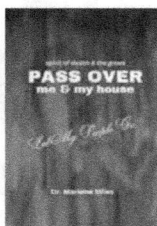

Throne of Grace: Courtroom Prayer
https://a.co/d/fNMxcM9

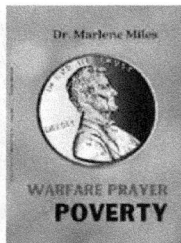

Warfare Prayer Against Poverty
https://a.co/d/bZ61lYu

Other books by this author

AK: *The Adventures of the Agape Kid*

AMONG SOME THIEVES

Ancestral Powers https://a.co/d/9prTyFf

Backstabbers https://a.co/d/gi8iBxf

Barrenness, *Prayers Against*
https://a.co/d/feUltIs

Battlefield of Marriage, *The*

Blindsided: *Has the Old Man Bewitched You?* https://a.co/d/5O2fLLR

Break Free from Collective Captivity

Casting Down Imaginations
https://a.co/d/1UxlLqa

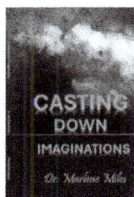

Churchcraft: Witchcraft In the Church

Churchzilla, The Wanna-Be, Supposed-to-be Bride of Christ

Curses of Blind Men

Demonic Cobwebs (prayerbook)

Demonic Time Bombs

Demons Hate Questions

Devil Loves Trauma, *The*

Devil Weapons: Unforgiveness, Bitterness,...

The Devourers: *Thieves of Darkness 2*

Do Not Swear by the Moon

Don't Refuse Me, Lord (4 book series)
https://a.co/d/idP34LG

Dream Defilement

The Emptiers: *Thieves of Darkness, 1*
https://a.co/d/5I4n5mc

Every Evil Arrow https://a.co/d/afgRkiA

Evil Touch https://a.co/d/gSGGpS1

Failed Assignment
https://a.co/d/3CXtjZY

Fantasy Spirit Spouse
https://a.co/d/hW7oYbX

FAT Demons (The): *Breaking Demonic Curses*

The Fold (5-book series)

- The Fold (Book 1)
- Name Your Seed (Book 2)
- The Poor Attitudes of Money (3)
- Do Not Orphan Your Seed (4)
- For the Sake of the Gospel (5)
- My Sowing Journal

Gang Ups: *Touch Not God's Anointed*

got HEALING? Verses for Life

got LOVE? Verses for Life

got HOPE? Verses for Life

got money? https://a.co/d/g2av41N

How to Dental Assist

How to Dental Assist2: Be Productive, Not Wasteful

I Take It Back

Legacy

Let Me Have A Dollar's Worth
https://a.co/d/h8F8XgE

Level the Playing Field

Living for the NOW of God

Lose My Location
https://a.co/d/crD6mV9

Love Breaks Your Heart

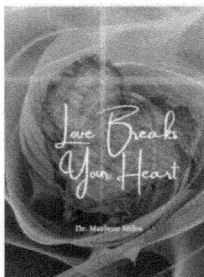

Man Safari, *The*

Marriage Ed. Rules of Engagement & Marriage

Made Perfect in Love

Money Hunters: Beware of Those

Money on the Altar https://a.co/d/4EqJ2Nr

Mulberry Tree https://a.co/d/9nR9rRb

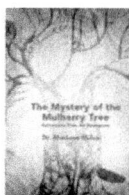

Motherboard (The) - *Soul Prosperity Series*

Name Your Seed

Occupy: *Until I Return*

Plantation Souls

Players Gonna Play

Power Money: Nine Times the Tithe

https://a.co/d/gRt41gy

The Power of Wealth *(forthcoming)*

Powers Above

Remember the Time https://a.co/d/3PbBjkF

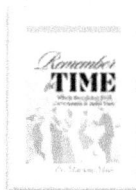

Repent of Visiting Evil Altars
https://a.co/d/3n3Zjwx

The Robe, *Part 1, The Lessons of Joseph*

The Robe, *The Lessons of Joseph* Part II,

Seasons of Grief

Seasons of Waiting

Seasons of War

Second Marriage, Third~~, *Any Marriage*
https://a.co/d/6m6GN4N

Seducing Spirits: *Idolatry & Whoredoms*

Sift You Like Wheat

Six Men Short: What Has Happened to all the Men?

Soul Prosperity, Soul Prosperity Series Book 3
https://a.co/d/5p8YvCN

Soulish & Diabolical Prayer Treatment

Souls In Captivity, Soul Prosperity Series Book 2

The Spirit of Poverty

StarStruck

SUNBLOCK

The Swallowers: *Thieves of Darkness*, Book 3

Take It Back

This Is NOT That: How to Keep Demons from Coming at You

Time Is of the Essence

Too Many Wives: *Why You Have Lady Problems*

Tormenting Spirits   https://a.co/d/dAogEJf

Toxic Souls

Triangular Power *(series)*

- Powers Above
- SUNBLOCK
- Do Not Swear by the Moon
- STARSTRUCK

Uncontested Doom

Unguarded Hours, *The*

Unseen Life, *The* https://a.co/d/0drZ5Ll

Upgrade: How to Get Out of Survival Mode

- Toxic Souls (Book 2 of series)

- Legacy (Book 3 of series)

The Wasters: *Thieves of Darkness,* Bk 2
https://a.co/d/bUvI9Jo

What Have You to Declare? What Do You Have With You from Where You've Been?

When I Was A Child, *I Prayed As a Child*

When the Devourer is Rebuked

https://a.co/d/1HVv8oq

The Wilderness Romance *(series)* This series is about conducting a Godly relationship and marriage with someone who is a Wilderness person. It is about how to recognize it and navigate through it. These books are about how not to get caught up in such.

- *The Social Wilderness*
- *The Sexual Wilderness*
- *The Spiritual Wilderness*

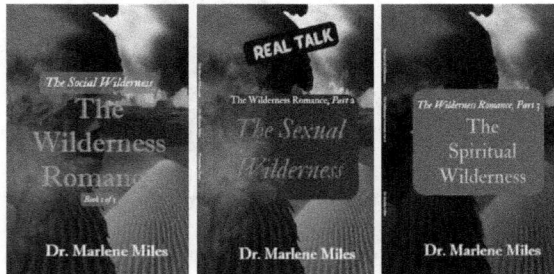

Other Series

The Fold (a series on Godly finances)
https://a.co/d/4hz3unj

Soul Prosperity Series https://a.co/d/bz2M42q

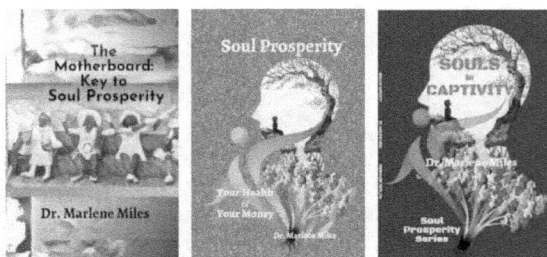

Spirit Spouse books

https://a.co/d/9VehDSo

https://a.co/d/97sKOwm

Thieves of Darkness series

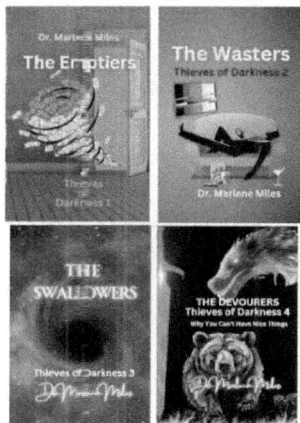

Triangular Powers https://a.co/d/aUCjAWC

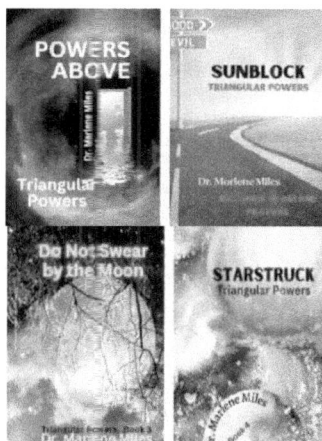

Upgrade (series) *How to Get Out of Survival Mode* https://a.co/d/aTERhX0

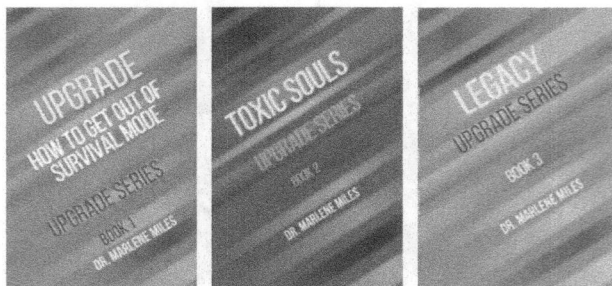

www.ingramcontent.com/pod-product-compliance
Lightning Source LLC
LaVergne TN
LVHW021353080426
835508LV00020B/2265